YANIS DELANEY

YOUR COLLEGE EXPERIENCE

The Ultimate Guide to Finding The Ideal University For You,
Learn Expert Tips and Advice on How to Choose the Right
Education Institution That Would Shape Your Future

Descrierea CIP a Bibliotecii Naţionale a României
YANIS DELANEY
   YOUR COLLEGE EXPERIENCE. The Ultimate Guide to Finding The Ideal University For You, Learn Expert Tips and Advice on How to Choose the Right Education Institution That Would Shape Your Future. / Yanis Delaney – Bucharest: Editura My Ebook, 2021
   ISBN

YANIS DELANEY

YOUR COLLEGE EXPERIENCE

The Ultimate Guide to Finding The Ideal University For You, Learn Expert Tips and Advice on How to Choose the Right Education Institution That Would Shape Your Future

My Ebook Publishing House
Bucharest, 2021

TABLE OF CONTENTS

FOREWORD

They say that one's success greatly depends on numerous things, such as knowledge, skills, perseverance, and determination, just to name a few. But do you know that choosing the right education institution also plays a major role when it comes to shaping your future?

If you happen to be one of the millions of students who are still undecided on what university or college you will enter, then, this book is something that you need to read right now.

Learn how you should choose a university based on different factors and be able to improve your chances in reaching the kind of success that you have been dreaming of.

Ideal University

Shaping Your Future Through the Right Education Institution

CHAPTER 1

WHY THE RIGHT UNIVERSITY
IS IMPORTANT FOR YOUR FUTURE?

Synopsis

Aside from their own talents and skills, the future of today's students is also dependent upon the university or educational institution that they choose to join. Why is it important for you to choose the right university? In this chapter, learn the effect of being a part of a top university to your future success.

Is it really that important to attend one of today's top universities to make the most money in the future and be successful in your chosen career?

Without a doubt, some of the elite colleges such as Dartmouth and the top universities like Princeton carry a name recognition which will be able to help you in securing an interview or winning a job despite a high number of other candidates. But why is it so?

Choose the Right University and Change Your Future for the Better

Why is choosing the right university really influential when it comes to changing your future and ensuring your success in the field that you have chosen?

Better Networking Opportunities

Attending the right university, especially the top ones, will be able to help you in building influential networks which can open various doors of opportunities even right after your graduation.

Both the alumni and faculty members will be able to help you in obtaining job leads and references, and on top of that, you will also be able to establish an extensive network of friends coming from various walks of life that can eventually lead to a higher number of job opportunities.

Aside from these, the seminars and conferences held at the top universities will also give you the chance of getting in touch with specialists and experts that can help you in securing internships as well as full time employment.

How Will You Determine the Right University?

It is not enough that you just choose the right university but instead, you need to look for the best one that will meet all your needs: academic, financial, career, and more importantly, personal.

If you have already determined the specific career that you would like to pursue, then, choosing a university that specializes in the field that you want or has outstanding academic programs in your chosen field can give you the chance of graduating fully equipped and prepared to face the tough job market.

For example, there are several universities that contain nursing colleges, journalism schools or schools of information science and library. Also, there are some independent professional institutions like law schools, art schools, and the veterinary universities.

Finding the Best University That Suits You

Being a graduate of one of the best universities will help guarantee success but you also have to remember that this is solely where your future lies. at the end of the day, your career and academic achievements will still greatly depend more on your determination and hard work more than the school's name recognition.

Aside from that, the value of university education encompasses not only potential earning power and career success. Students will be able to achieve a lot of intangible benefits from their experiences, which include the opportunity of expanding their worldviews, establishing lifelong friendships, participating in various activities and studying abroad.

Furthermore, based on research, university graduates have the tendency of having higher rates when it comes to civic participation and what is even better is that they are more likely to become happy individuals in general.

CHAPTER 2

PAYING A VISIT TO THE UNIVERSITY DURING ITS OPEN DAY

Synopsis

Do you want to get a glimpse of a university where you are planning to enroll? Then, paying a visit during its open day is the best thing that you can do. So, what are the things that you have to remember to make this short and limited visit a worthwhile and meaningful one? Learn more about a university's open day in this chapter.

Make the Most Out of Open Days – Visiting Your Prospect Universities

Open days – this is the time of sheer excitement when universities try to present themselves in the best light as well as outshine their competitors. However, aside from the universities, the experience during open days is useful for parents and more importantly, the students themselves.

Today, open days have become more important than the universities, with students checking out an extensive list of universities. Before, they only visit 2 or 3 but these days, it has increased to 6 or 7. There are even instances when they visit one university over and over again, like they are newlyweds searching for their very first home.

The open days are now more professional than ever. They have been deconstructed, with universities thinking about each point of "experience," starting from arriving, up to parking, as well as meeting the ambassador guides, with the entire staff being fully briefed on the possible questions and the like.

Visiting universities during open days can be very thrilling and to make the most out of this exciting experience, there are things that you need to do for it to be a great day.

- Never forget the postcode. This thing is very easy to do but unfortunately, many tend to forget it, thus ruining their experience during open days.

- While your antennae might be sharper if you attend the open day all on your own, it might still be useful if there is another set of watchful eyes to observe the environment and check if it will be suitable for you or not.

- Is the area something that you can stand? Open days are not solely about your chosen course because these things can be easily searched online. More importantly, these events are about whether or not you can live and stay in one place for several years. Try to imagine how it feels to be there when the rain is pouring heavily or when the sun is too scorching up in the sky.

- How about the accommodation? Is it properly allocated? What will happen after your initial year? What are the best halls and which are those that are simply worth avoiding?

- If you will use the open days for shortlisting your university choices, ask yourself if you will really be enrolling there once you get an offer. Never choose a "safety" that you will regret in the end.

- Make sure that you get your questions ready, although many of them will not really be answered if you will ask around and you have more chances of getting them solved when you check the university site, but still. Who are the teachers of undergraduates – post-grads or professors? What are used for assessing the course? Is it by coursework, class participation, coursework or exams only?

These are only some of the things that you might want to take into consideration when you visit your prospect universities on their open days. Keep them in mind in order to make the most out of this visit and for you to come up with the best decision in the end.

CHAPTER 3

DECIDING BASED ON THE SPECIALTY
OF THE UNIVERSITY

Synopsis

Every university has its own field of specialization and if you are currently undecided as to which one you should choose, you need to consider your own preferences in order for you to pick a university that will best suit you. Whether you are interested in business, art, law or any other fields of specialty, you will surely find it easy to look for the best university appropriate for the career that you want to pursue in the future.

While it is true that all educational institutions offer various courses and majors to their students, they also happen to have their own specialties, and this is yet another important factor that you need to consider during your search.

Look for Universities That Suit Your Chosen Field

Whether you choose to study on top and long established universities like the University of Oxford, Cambridge University, Harvard University, Massachusetts Institute of Technology, Princeton University, and others or you rather stay in low profile but still good institutions, you will have to take into account the specific major that you are planning to take and if the university that you will choose is known for that particular field.

This is a way of ensuring that you will get the most out of your major and you will stay at the forefront of other graduates when you apply after you have graduated.

For example, if you want to pursue a major in business, the University of Oxford can be your best choice. As a well known public university, it is recognized as among the oldest university that is said to have been established way back in the 11th century.

If you want to pursue veterinary medicine, one of the well known names in the field is Cornell University. For those who are looking for top ranked engineering programs, California State Polytechnic University might also be worth considering.

There are simply tons and tons of universities and the only thing that you need to do is conduct a research in order for you to learn about their specialties.

CHAPTER 4

LOCATION & ENVIRONMENT
OF THE UNIVERSITY

Synopsis

Two of the most crucial things that you need to consider when looking for a good university are the location and environment. Is it safe? Is it close to your home? Would there be sufficient amenities? Is it accessible to different modes of transportation? These and many more are factors that you have to take into account during your search for a good university.

Environment and Location – How Important Are They? The university that you will choose will serve as your home for the whole 4 or even more years of your education. This is the reason why you need to search for one whose environment and location perfectly meets all your needs and requirements.

In the case of some students, different personal factors like distance from family and friends limit the location of the universities they apply to.

However, there are also those who do not take it as a factor in their decision at all.

But wherever you belong, there are several things that you need to ask yourself in order to narrow your list of choices.

What are the Geographic Regions That You Prefer?

Is there a particular geographic location where you prefer to stay or one that you want to avoid at all cost? Here, weather might be one of the essential factors to consider? Are you not a big fan of the cold? Do you like a school that is close enough to a sunny beach that you can easily go to on the weekends?

How Far Would You Like to Be From Your Home?

Would you like to go home during weekends to enjoy your favorite home cooked meals or do the laundry perhaps? Or would you rather be as far from home as possible? Are there friends in your home town that you like to meet regularly?

It is important for you to figure out your comfort zone as far as location is concerned. Everyone has the tendency to get homesick during the first year in college but most students overcome it after the first semester. It will all be up to you on how close or far you would like to be from your home.

Is It Accessible By Different Means of Transportation?

If your chosen university is far from your home, you will also need to consider how you are going to travel to and fro the campus as well as the possible cost of this. For short distances, you can make them by care but if it is far from your home, you might need to ride a train, bus or even travel by air. Think how often you will be returning home for visits, factoring in the costs and travel time.

Considering the University Environment

Aside from the location, the environment of the school itself is also important to take into account. It should be something that is friendly to students and will promote better study habits. The amenities of the university that you will choose should also be sufficient and suitable to your chosen major. For instance, if you are a music major, there should be adequate and functional musical instruments for every person in your class. If you will study studio arts, inquire if there is practice or studio availability and if there is enough locker space for all your instruments and personal supplies.

CHAPTER 5

CHOOSING THE UNIVERSITY
YOU CAN AFFORD

Synopsis

When searching for a university, being a wise student, financially speaking, is a must. Obviously, you can never enroll in one that you cannot afford and will make you neck-deep in debts even before you have graduated. How will you choose an affordable university? Here are some things that you have to bear in mind.

Be Smart in Your Educational Choices

You have already found a university that you love and you just cannot wait to get enrolled and start your life as a part of the place. But in your rush to attending the school that you like, were you really able to carry out due diligence on your decision making?

While you might be aware of all the available campus amenities, degree options, as well as job placement assistance, do you also know if you can afford being in that school? Is your budget enough for your expenses during your entire stay there to complete the program or degree that you have chosen, and not only for one semester or one year?

Below are several suggestions to help you choose a university that you can easily afford.

Calculate Your Education's Actual Cost

To know if your chosen university is something that you can afford, you should start by calculating your education's actual cost. Try to add up in advance all the expenses that you will have, like tuition, school, fees, living expenses and books before you factor in all the available financial aid, like grants, scholarship, student loans and work-study.

By doing so, you can have a "ballpark" estimate of your expenses in order for you to get a truer and more accurate cost. Of course, you will not really be able to know the exact cost that you will spend out of your pocket until you have been finally admitted to the university and you got the award letter for the financial aid that you will get but still, calculating the cost can give you a good enough rough estimate.

"Safety" School vs. "Reach" School

Majority of students do not completely understand the concept of a "safety" school versus "reach" school as far as the academic criteria is concerned.

You choose your favorite universities and then you hope that you will get in. However, it is also important that you consider applying to back up schools if ever you have not been accepted to the school of your first choice. You might want to apply in the same way to schools, financially speaking. A back up plan should be ready if ever you have been admitted to your favorite school but you cannot afford it or you do not like acquiring a lot of debts as needed, depending on the financial aid package offered by the school.

When you plan ahead and you pick a university that you will be able to afford, there is a higher chance that you will be able to successfully complete the degree or program in order for you to see the perfect return on your investment. Take note that your expenses for your education are a great investment that you will make for yourself as well as your ability of earning much more in the near future so make sure that you invest wisely!

CHAPTER 6

LOOKING FOR UNIVERSITY
THAT PROVIDES FINANCIAL AID

Synopsis

Many universities today offer their students with financial aid in order to give them the chance of completing their chosen degrees and being able to reach all their goals and dreams. How should you look for these universities that provide financial assistance to their students? Learn this and more in this chapter.

Look for Good Financial Aid Packages

To help their students in finishing their studies without the need to be burdened by all the school expenses, different universities offer financial aid packages that can greatly help in reducing the total cost of going to college.

During your search for a school that offers their students with financial aid, the best resort that you've got is to check their official website in order for you to learn about their requirements.

Right now, many students are supported by these packages and most of them were able to get one by simply following the set requirements of the schools.

While the overall college cost is one crucial factor that you have to take into consideration, this must not be your sole focus until later in the process of choosing a university. Instead, your attention should be on finding a school that is a great fit, something that will be able to meet your academic, personal and career needs.

There are cases when receiving a financial aid has higher chances if you will apply to a private college, making you pay for a much lower overall price compared to that of a public institution. This is because most private colleges today offer more financial aid packages in order to get the interest of more students coming from various income levels.

At the end of the day, researching ahead of time is yet again the key in order for you to get the financial aid that will suit your needs.

CHAPTER 7

CONSIDERATIONS FOR CHOOSING
A UNIVERSITY ABROAD

Synopsis

Studying abroad can be a truly exciting experience for many students. The thought of being in a different place with different people and entirely different culture and tradition is certainly a risk worth taking. If you have plans to study in a different country, there are several things that you have to consider when choosing a university abroad.

Right now, there is an extensive plethora of universities that proffer exciting opportunities for the students to continue their education on a foreign land. Many students choose to study in universities abroad for the purpose of fulfilling their fancies of full degree or exchange year programs. Studying abroad provide students with an entirely different teaching approach, a different way of living their life, an inter-cultural mix as well as a multitude of wonderful benefits.

Factors to Consider When Looking for Universities Abroad

Earning a degree overseas can definitely add a different glitter to your currently vitae, enhancing your chances of financial and career growth. However, there are a few factors that you need to consider prior to coming up with a decision as to which overseas university you should choose.

A few of these considerations include the country where you plan to study, the possible consequences if you choose a certain university abroad, the field where you want to major, the expectations of a certain country and university, the choice of residence, whether in your own arrangement or within the campus and above anything else, the financial concerns.

Once you have finished answering the questions as honestly as you can, you will be able to get an in-depth know-how of the universities abroad. The place where you plan to study is a must when you look for an overseas school. This is the reason why you should not let yourself get swayed by the cool weather and picturesque landscape and instead, make sure that you pick a college that ranks high on your personal anticipations. Some of the crucial factors that are encompassed in the context of the place of study include the scholarships offered, the course program, the faculties' experience, research scope, and others.

Once you have decided on these factors, the next thing that you can shift your attention to include the recreational activities, like the scope of the available part time jobs, vacation opportunities, cultural mix, and others. Another factor will be the assistance that educational consultancies give to the students that choose to study abroad. They are the ones who have exact figures and facts about the placement success, the reviews of former students and other available assistance. They can provide you with some insider tricks, tips and the suitable reaction to your dilemmas and queries.

See to it that you have the right eligibility about the previous academic scores, sufficient TOEFL, cat or GMAT scores, previous work experience and others. Universities abroad aptly gauge your entire persona which is why you will also need to improve both your character and your overall personality. Your cultural experience when you study in a university abroad is also very important. You can get the perfect chance of meeting new folks and discovering brand new language, food, rituals, music and dance. The financial concerns of studying in a university overseas also hold an extreme significance.

If you feel that your resources are not enough for sustaining the entire structure of the fees, you can always search for good scholarships. A few of the best ways for you to save enough money when you study abroad include finding roommates or paying a guest accommodation to reduce your expenses on accommodation.

It will also be a much better idea if you choose to cook your own food instead of dining the restaurants or cafeterias. Make sure that you also keep updated with your home country's currency value as against to that of the country where you study as this will give you a great sense of assessment and provide you with the response on the state of your finances every now and then.

Studying in universities abroad can definitely become a more worthwhile and exclusive experience when you remember all these factors.

CHAPTER 8

PERFORM SOME RESEARCH ONLINE
FOR UNIVERSITY YOU'RE INTENDED TO JOIN

Synopsis

With the help of the internet, learning more about the university that you are planning to join has become much easier than ever. Today, you can now perform some research online to discover if a certain university is really the one that you are looking for. In this chapter, discover more about the things that you can get from performing an online research.

When looking for the right university, it is a must that you consider the things that are most important to you for this is the best way of weeding out the schools in your list which are completely unrealistic or do not have the qualities that you assume essential on your intended school. Think about the things that you would like to get out of your university experience, whether the institution has an established academic record, diverse social services and programs, outstanding athletic teams and identify if you are applying to universities for the right reasons.

Choose the Right School – Research Online Today

The moment you have applied and accepted, you need to compare their offered packages for financial aid for this decision might call for more sacrifices than what you made when you are deciding where you should apply. Identify if it is worth it to take out several student loans at a certain school and if ever it is, try to create an action plan that you can use for getting the best out of the free money in grants and scholarships that you can.

Set Aside the Reputation

Each college application must have one dream school included in their list which can be slightly out of their reach, either academically or financially. But together with that one application for the dream school, high school seniors bound to college must look at the schools which can offer them either a kind of program that they would to pursue or an extensive range of programs that they can pick from in case you are undecided.

36

If you are already sure about the career that you want, there are several smaller and less expensive universities are known for specific schools, and this is where it is important for you to perform an online research regarding those institutions specializing in your chosen field. Set aside everything that you head regarding the schools, the word of mouth coming from the older brother of your friend and try looking beyond what you think will impress the members of your family or will look great on your resume. There is just a wide range of universities out there that has superb academic programs which might turn out to be more impressive compared to those large and expensive universities that the rest of your classmates are vying for.

Considerations for the Cost

You might want to consider the low cost choices if you are concerned as to how you will pay back the student loans that you need to take out if you will choose to join a more expensive school. See to it that you also compare out of state college costs with that of in state tuitions when you decide on the short list of the universities that you will apply to. Depending on the place of your residence, you might still enjoy the experience of going to college and still maintain that sense of independence with no need to leave the state and enjoy the wonderful cost benefits of studying locally. And if ever you will not feel homesick during the first year, it is going to be easier and even less expensive on your part to visit your home compared to if you will make a long move across the country.

While state grants and scholarships have become common, usually, they can only go to those long time residents of a certain state as a means of boosting the local economy and keeping qualified applicants from leaving their own home states.

While it can be tough to choose the right university for you, by simply performing an online search, you will surely be able to come up with an impressive list of schools which will not just meet your specific needs but at the same time, will be cost effective for you.

CHAPTER 9

CHECKING ON THE RANKING
OF THE UNIVERSITY

Synopsis

What is the role of a university's ranking on your decision making? Does the placement of a certain school against other schools mean a lot? Will it really reflect their overall standing? Check the ranking of your intended university and see if this is truly that important when you make your decision or not.

Do you know that although you should not put 100% weighting on university rankings, still, they can be a great tool when making an important decision in life like choosing a university where you will be spending the next few years for your education?

Impressions Matter – Check the University Rankings

University rankings happen to be most useful if you have plans to join one of the world's best institutions, although you might want to remember that these also happen to be the most competitive.

The rankings of universities by subject can be extremely helpful, assisting you to find the finest universities that suit your area of interest and at times, the ordering can be a bit different as compared to the general ranking.

Aside from looking at the rankings themselves, you also need to get yourself familiar with the methodology used behind them. It will explain how each university is assessed and why one ranks higher than another.

The personal criteria that you have might not necessarily be exactly similar with the ones used for the making of the ranking. For instance, you might consider international diversity or the university employer's reputation to be a big factor.

If there is a certain region in the world where you plan to study, you might also want to consult the regional rankings.

There is no denying that these numbers can greatly influence your decision in choosing a university but more than these rankings, you should still take into account all the other factors mentioned in the previous chapters to come up with an educated decision.

CHAPTER 10

ENTER UNIVERSITIES THAT COMPANIES OFTEN SOUGHT FOR EMPLOYEES

Synopsis

The last but definitely not the least thing that you have to consider if you really want to come up with the best decision on the university that you will join, you also have to determine if your chosen institutions are among those that companies usually sought for their potential employees. Why is it so?

Learn the answers in this chapter.

Whether you accept it or not, in this competitive world, only the fittest survive and as far as employment is concerned, aside from your outstanding grades, long list of commendations and achievements and an extensive citation of references, the name of the university where you came from is also considered by potential employers.

Search for a University In Demand Among Potential Employers

At first, this might seem like discrimination, especially since at most cases, the university or school itself has nothing to do with the knowledge and skills of an applicant.

However, at this point in time, more and more companies screen their applicants by basing on the name of the university or college cited on the curriculum vitae.

As it so happens, applicants that came from established, well known and top universities also tend to be the best in their field because the institutions where they spent their college years are fully dedicated in honing them to be the best that they can be, with the help of an experienced faculty, good study environment, state of the art amenities, and many other perks that, unfortunately, are not provided by those universities whose names might even be unheard of.

Remember that the ideal university is something that can help in shaping your future for the better and for this to happen, it should be an institution well known and familiar to those potential employers in the companies where you plan to pursue your career in the hopes of creating a brighter future ahead of.

By making the right choice of university, you will also be making the right path to take not only for your education but for your future as well.

Printed by Libri Plureos GmbH in Hamburg, Germany